H

595.7
Ben   Bender, Lionel

        Poisonous insects

Wah-wah-taysee, Wah-wah-taysee.

POISONOUS
INSECTS

Design
David West
Children's Book Design
Illustrations
George Thompson
Picture Research
Cecilia Weston-Baker
Editor
Denny Robson
Consultant
John Stidworthy

© Aladdin Books Ltd

Designed and produced by
Aladdin Books Ltd
70 Old Compton Street
London W1

*First published in the
United States in 1988 by*
Gloucester Press
387 Park Avenue South
New York NY 10016

Printed in Belgium

ISBN 0-531-17103-5
Library of Congress Catalog
Card Number 88-50510

This book tells you about many of the insects that cause harm or damage to other animals and to plants. It tells you where the insects live, what they look like and how they survive. Find out some surprising facts in the boxes on each page. The identification chart at the back will help you when you see these insects in zoos or in the wild.

The little square shows you the size of the insect. Each side represents 5cm (2in).

The picture opposite shows a Gum Moth Caterpillar

FIRST SIGHT

POISONOUS INSECTS

Lionel Bender

GLOUCESTER PRESS

New York · London · Toronto · Sydney

Introduction

Insects are one of the most successful groups of animals. There are over a million different species and they live in all parts of the world. Insects owe their success to several features. Most species have wings and can fly. They can move freely to find food or mates, or to escape their enemies. They have a hard waterproof outer covering, the exoskeleton. This provides protection and allows them to live in dry areas. They can also reproduce in great numbers.

Many insects are also equipped with weapons, both to frighten off attackers and to kill the animals on which they feed. Some produce poisons. Others sting their attackers or have nasty spines that can cause swelling and blistering of the skin.

Contents

◁ **The bright colours of Harlequin Bugs warn birds not to eat them**

The prickly spines of this Emperor Gum Moth Caterpillar are tipped with poison ▷

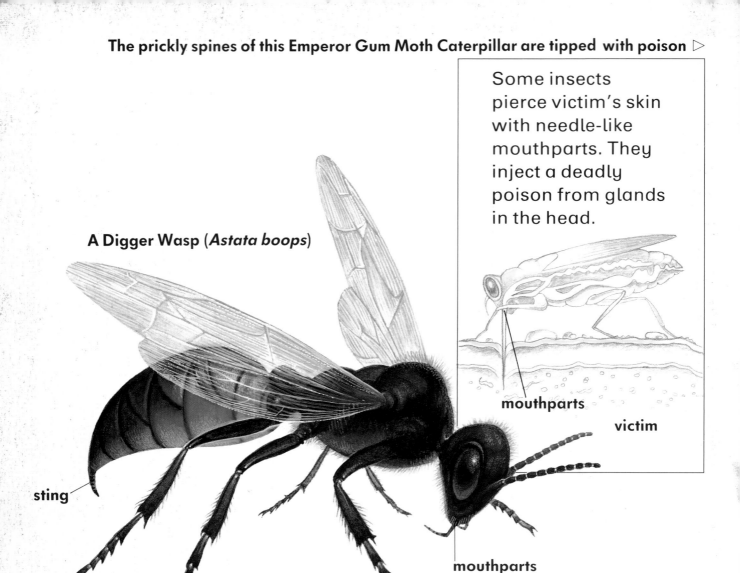

A Digger Wasp (*Astata boops*)

Some insects pierce victim's skin with needle-like mouthparts. They inject a deadly poison from glands in the head.

mouthparts

victim

sting

mouthparts

Insect weapons

All insects have specialised mouthparts. The Tsetse Fly feeds on the blood of mammals, including humans. It has piercing and sucking mouthparts. As the fly feeds, it injects saliva into the wound. The saliva contains tiny animals that produce harmful chemicals inside the victim's body. Assassin bugs have mouthparts with glands that produce a poison as the insects feed. The poison kills or stuns the victim.

At the rear of most insects' bodies is an egg or sperm tube. In female bees, wasps and ants, the tube has become a pointed sting that injects poison. Some insects possess poisonous chemicals inside their bodies.

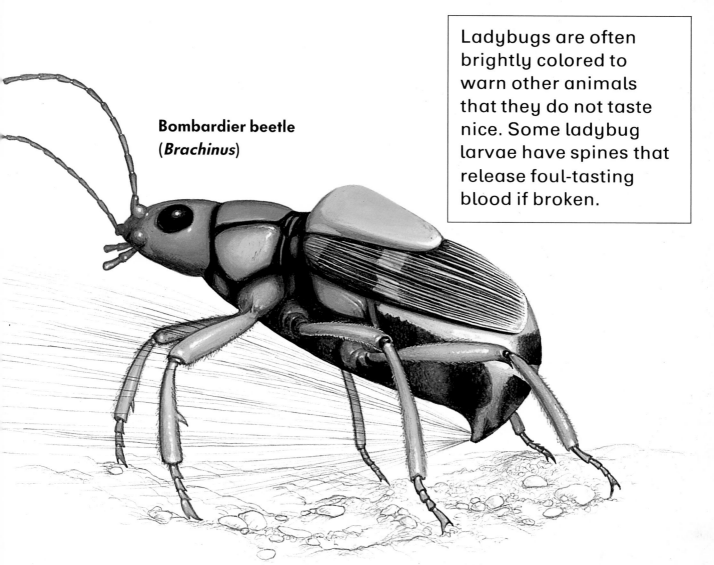

Bombardier beetle
(*Brachinus*)

Ladybugs are often brightly colored to warn other animals that they do not taste nice. Some ladybug larvae have spines that release foul-tasting blood if broken.

Bombardier and oil beetles

Bombardier beetles frighten off would-be attackers, such as ants, toads and mice, by spraying them with boiling hot liquids. The liquids cause the attacker's skin to swell up and become painful. The spray is shot out of the rear of the beetle's body through a fine nozzle. Some non-flying ground beetles squirt out acids when disturbed. These chemicals burn the skin and cause serious damage to the eyes of mammals.

Oil beetles store a poisonous chemical in their bodies. The larvae of some African leaf beetles are so poisonous that native people in the Kalahari Desert use them to tip their arrows when they hunt birds and large mammals.

◁ **The black and yellow markings of this Palm Beetle warn off predators**

Leaf and bark beetles

Each year, leaf-feeding beetles cause millions of dollars worth of damage to crops. They spread diseases from plant to plant so that seeds do not form. The beetles carry microscopic creatures — mostly bacteria (germs) — inside their bodies. The bacteria get into the plants as the insects feed. They produce poisons that prevent plants from growing properly.

Female bark beetles bore into the wood of trees to lay their eggs. These beetles carry a tiny fungus that causes a deadly disease in the trees. When the beetle larvae hatch, they chew out tunnels in the wood. At the same time the fungus clogs up the tubes which carry the trees' sap. The tree dies within only a few weeks.

Oak Bark Beetle (*Scolytus vitricatus*)

Dutch elm disease is caused by a fungus carried by the Elm Bark Beetle. The larvae tunnel through the wood. When adult, they bore through the bark of the tree and fly off.

◁ **The Colorado Beetle, although not poisonous itself, destroys crops**

Termites and leaf insects

Termites are probably best known for the giant mounds of earth they build. The mounds house their colonies of millions of eggs, larvae and adults. But snouted termites are also well known for the sticky and irritating chemicals they produce to defend themselves against ants, their arch enemies. The soldier termites squirt the chemicals from their snouts.

Leaf and stick insects are shaped and colored to blend in with their surroundings. Usually they go unnoticed by animals that eat insects. But if they are disturbed, some of them squirt their attackers with digested food. This contains acids that burn their victims' skin and eyes.

A leaf insect is poised to squirt irritating chemicals

Soldier Snouted Termites protect two fellow worker termites ▷

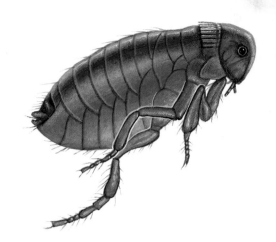

Fleas spread diseases because they reproduce in great numbers and they can move easily from victim to victim. The Human Flea can travel 30cm (12in) with each leap.

Fleas and lice

Fleas and lice survive by feeding on other living creatures. Some attack people, pets and farm animals to suck their blood. The Human Body Louse has mouthparts that include a needle-like hollow tube. This can pierce a person's skin and the blood is sucked through it. The insect's jab causes irritation. As the person scratches his or her skin, a germ which may be carried by the louse gets into the body. This causes an unpleasant disease called typhus.

In the 14th and 16th centuries, the Rat Flea was responsible for the deaths of millions of people throughout Europe. The flea can carry a germ from rats to people. This germ produces a poison causing a disease known as the Black Death, or bubonic plague.

A Human Flea jumping

Bugs

Bugs are insects with piercing and sucking mouthparts which are housed in a long beak-like structure. Assassin bugs hunt and feed on other insects. A few produce scents to attract bees. They seize the bees with their forelegs and inject a poisonous saliva into them. They can also squirt the saliva at attackers. Other assassin bugs are called kissing bugs because they often bite people in the face and inject a poison.

Shield bugs feed on plants. They are often brightly colored and have strange shapes. This warns other animals that they have poisonous chemicals in their bodies and are not to be eaten.

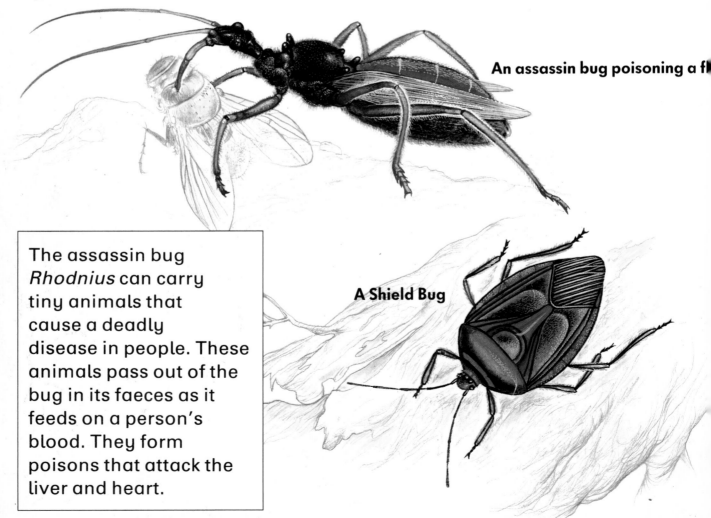

An assassin bug poisoning a fl[

A Shield Bug

The assassin bug *Rhodnius* can carry tiny animals that cause a deadly disease in people. These animals pass out of the bug in its faeces as it feeds on a person's blood. They form poisons that attack the liver and heart.

An assassin bug sinks its needle-like mouthparts into a Shield Bug ▷

A female *Anopheles* mosquito in the act of taking a blood meal from a human

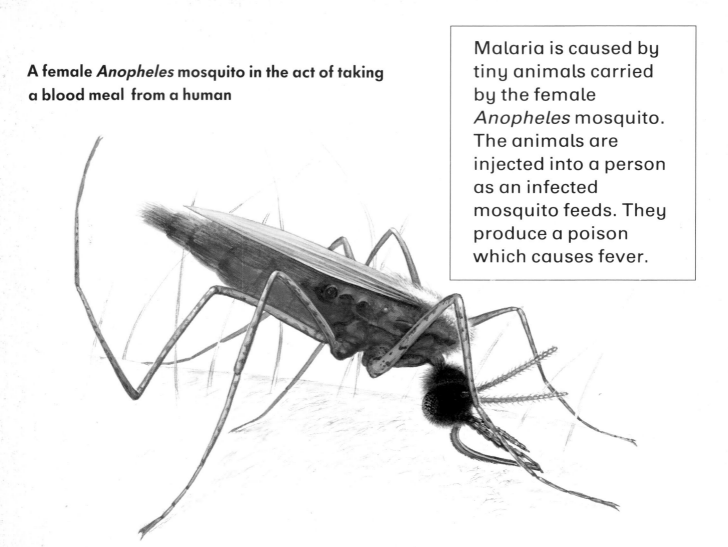

Malaria is caused by tiny animals carried by the female *Anopheles* mosquito. The animals are injected into a person as an infected mosquito feeds. They produce a poison which causes fever.

Flies

True flies have one pair of wings. They also have sucking mouthparts and feed on liquid foods of all kinds, from nectar to blood. They do not produce poisons themselves, but they carry germs that can cause illness and damage in other living creatures. The Malaria Mosquito causes the death of at least one million people every year in Africa and Asia. Tsetse Flies can cause a disease called sleeping sickness.

Bluebottles and houseflies love to eat rotting meat and fresh animal droppings. As they do so, they pick up germs on their mouthparts and feet. When the insects land on food in our homes, they leave the germs behind. If we eat the food, the germs can cause stomach upsets.

A Tsetse Fly rests on the surface of a person's skin and injects its saliva ▷

Butterflies and moths

Adult butterflies and moths can fly away from danger. But the caterpillars are easy prey. To protect themselves, many caterpillars have weapons. Others collect poisons from the plants they eat and store them inside their bodies. In some species, the poisons remain in the adults.

The Puss Moth Caterpillar warns off its enemies by showing its "face" markings when disturbed. It can also squirt an acid at an attacker. Slug caterpillars have tufts of sharp stinging hairs coated with poisons which can cause pain and swelling. Caterpillars of the South American Emperor Moth can inject a poison which causes serious bleeding.

The poisonous rear of the larva of the Death's Head Hawk Moth warns off predators

The Monarch Butterfly takes up chemicals from plants and makes itself poisonous to eat ▷

Ants and sawflies

Soldier ants guard an ant colony's nest. Most soldier ants have mouthparts and poisons that can be used to fight off attackers. A nip with the jaws of a soldier Black Bulldog Ant can kill an adult human within 15 minutes. Among Wood Ants and Army Ants, the soldiers can spray acids as a means of defense. One of these acids is called formic acid. It causes a painful burning sensation if sprayed into the eyes.

Sawfly larvae look like caterpillars. Those of the Australian Sawfly *Perga* feed only on the leaves of eucalyptus trees. They collect a foul-smelling chemical from the leaves. If the larvae are disturbed, they squirt the chemical from their mouths.

Sawfly larvae wave their poisonous bodies in a threat display

A Wood Ant produces a droplet of acid from its rear ▷

Hunting wasps

Wasps will sting people if threatened, but they are also useful insects. Many hunt and kill insect pests, such as caterpillars. Hunting wasps live alone and not in large swarms — they are not social insects. The females use their stings to capture other insects and spiders in order to feed their larvae.

A female Thread-waisted Wasp builds a nest in loose earth. Then she hunts for a caterpillar and paralyzes it with her sting. She drags the live caterpillar back to her nest using her legs. She lays an egg on her victim and closes up the nest entrance with small stones. When the wasp larva hatches, it feeds on the paralyzed caterpillar.

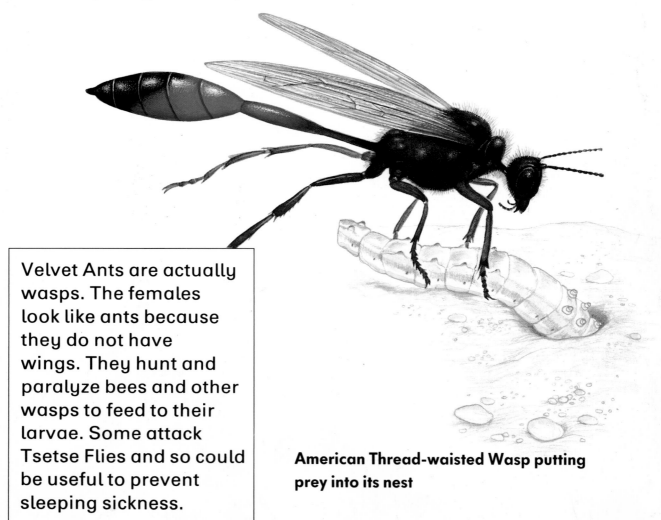

Velvet Ants are actually wasps. The females look like ants because they do not have wings. They hunt and paralyze bees and other wasps to feed to their larvae. Some attack Tsetse Flies and so could be useful to prevent sleeping sickness.

American Thread-waisted Wasp putting prey into its nest

◁ **A hunting wasp has successfully poisoned a tarantula**

Bees

Bees are also useful insects — they carry pollen from flower to flower to make fruit grow. But a bee's sting can sometimes be deadly. One person attacked by wild bees was stung 2,243 times and recovered. Recently in South and Central America, however, a type of bee has developed that has killed more than 150 people, each time with just a single sting.

The Honey Bee has a poisonous sting that it uses only in self-defense. The poison causes swelling and pain. The sting has tiny hooks that prevent the bee from pulling it out of its attacker. Soon after the bee uses its sting it dies. Bumble bees do not have a hooked sting and can use their sting many times.

Stinging Mason Bees build a nest of mud

Worker bees use their stings to defend themselves and the hive's queen ▷

Survival file

Poisonous insects such as the Malaria Mosquito and Elm Bark Beetle are pests. They are harmful to plants and animals. People often try to kill such insects by spraying them with chemicals called insecticides. But these chemicals kill all insects. Some insects are extremely helpful. Honey bees pollinate flowers, produce honey that we eat, and create waxes that we use to make candles and polishes. Ants and termites help in the breakdown of dead animal and plant material, which helps to make the soil rich and fertile.

A beekeeper wears protective clothing to prevent being stung

Because insecticides affect all insects, scientists are looking at other ways of killing insect pests. One way is to actually use poisonous insects. In some tree plantations, ladybugs have been introduced to get rid of aphids and scales. These are insects that feed on leaves, fruits and soft stems and so weaken the trees.

In parts of the United States, the Seven-spot Ladybug is used to control aphids that destroy potato plants by sucking up the plants' juices. Also in the United States the larvae of houseflies, which as adults contaminate fresh food, are used to control bark beetles and weevils that feed on crops.

This hunting wasp injects its larvae into the larvae of wasps that feed on trees

Ladybugs feed on aphids

Probably the most useful insects for pest control are the hunting wasps. More than 180 different species are being used around the world today to control the numbers of harmful and nuisance insects. Many species of hunting wasp prey on only one or two specific insects, such as certain caterpillars. So farmers can introduce a particular species of hunting wasp to kill a pest that is damaging a crop.

Identification chart

This chart shows you some of the poisonous insects described in this book. Some of them you can see in gardens, parks and farmland. To see others you will have to go to a zoo. Each square of the grid represents 10mm (0.4in).

- ○ Australia
- ○ Europe
- ● Africa
- ● Asia
- ● America

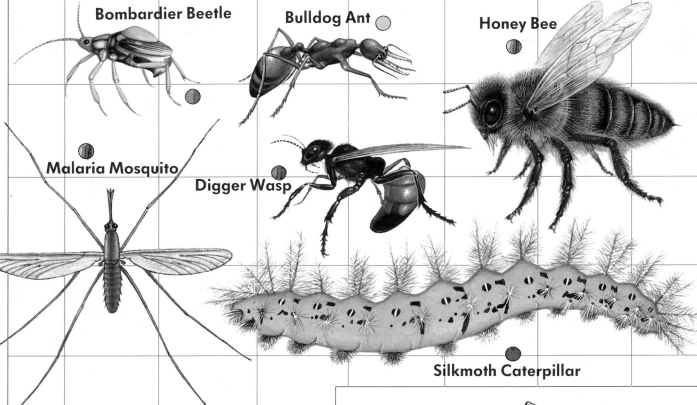

Bombardier Beetle

Bulldog Ant ○

Honey Bee

Malaria Mosquito

Digger Wasp

Silkmoth Caterpillar

Make your own stinging insect

A. Trace these shapes onto cardboard and cut them out.

B. Carefully glue and pin the parts together as shown.

C. When the insect has been put together, the head section can be turned so that the abdomen moves and the stinger shows.

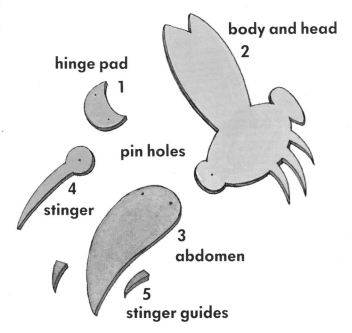

hinge pad
1

body and head
2

pin holes

4
stinger

3
abdomen

5
stinger guides

30

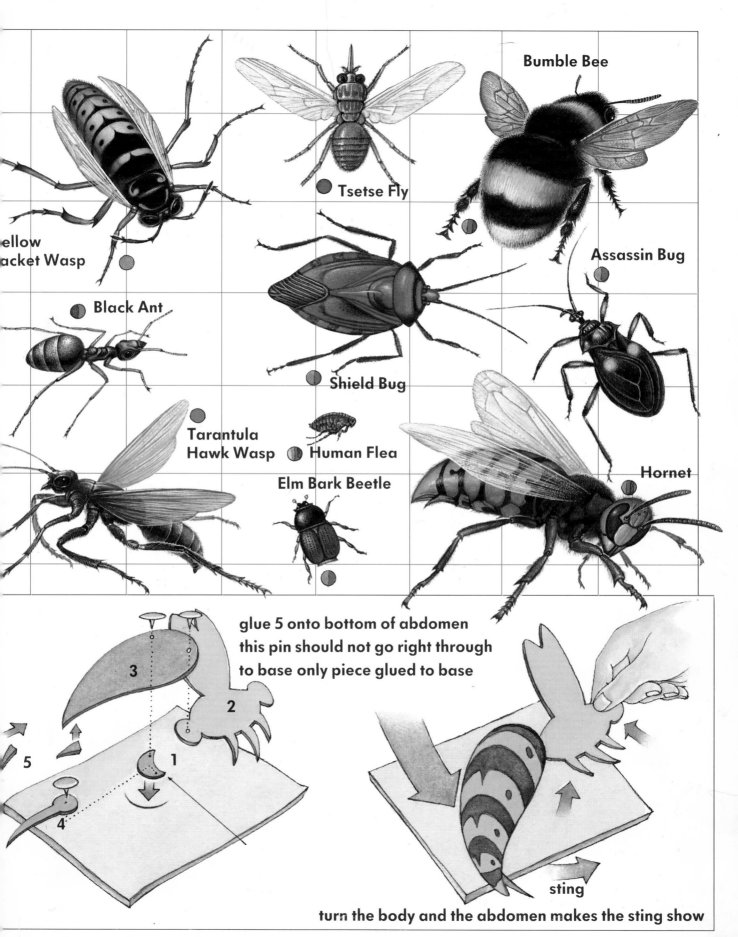

Bumble Bee

Tsetse Fly

ellow acket Wasp

Assassin Bug

Black Ant

Shield Bug

Tarantula Hawk Wasp

Human Flea

Hornet

Elm Bark Beetle

glue 5 onto bottom of abdomen
this pin should not go right through
to base only piece glued to base

sting

turn the body and the abdomen makes the sting show

31

Index

Photographic Credits:
Cover, title page and pages 4, 12, 13, 17, 19, 20, 21, 22, 23, 24, 28 and 29 (left): Bruce Coleman; pages 7, 8 and 29 (right): Planet Earth; page 15: Ardea.